49 (WEST RIDING) RECONNAISSANCE REGIMENT
ROYAL ARMOURED CORPS

Summary of Operations
June 1944 to May 1945

The Naval & Military Press Ltd

Published by

The Naval & Military Press Ltd
Unit 5 Riverside
Bellbrook Industrial Estate
Uckfield, East Sussex
TN22 1QQ England

Tel: +44 (0) 1825 749494
www.naval-military-press.com

Cover image: The British Army in North-west Europe 1944-45 Universal Carriers of 49th (West Riding) Division's Reconnaissance Regiment are welcomed by Dutch civilians on the outskirts of Kampen, 19 April 1945.

In reprinting in facsimile from the original, any imperfections are inevitably reproduced and the quality may fall short of modern type and cartographic standards.

SUMMARY OF OPERATIONS
MAPS
Scale 1/100,000

GSGS 4249	Sheet 7 F	CAEN – FALAISE
GSGS 4249	Sheet 8 E	LE HAVRE
GSGS 4249	Sheet 8 F	LISIEUX
GSGS 4249	Sheet 9 E	ROUEN
GSGS 4336	Sheet 3	ANTWERPEN
GSGS 4336	Sheet 4	MAESEYCK
GSGS 2541	Sheet 2	UTRECHT
GSGS 2541	Sheet 2 A	DEN HELDER
GSGS 2541	Sheet 4	ROTTERDAM
GSGS 2541	Sheet 5	's-HERTOGENBOSCH
GSGS 4416	Sheet P 1	BOCHOLT
GSGS 4416	Sheet N 2	OSNABRÜCK

Scale 1/250,000

GSGS 2738	Sheet 3 A & 8	CAEN & CHERBOURG
GSGS 4042	Sheet 2 A & 3 A	WALCHEREN-AMSTERDAM
GSGS 4042	Sheet 2	LILLE – GENT
GSGS 4042	Sheet 3	BRUSSELS – LIEGE
GSGS 4042	Sheet 4	LE HAVRE – AMIENS
GSGS 4042	Sheet 5	ARRAS – MONS
GSGS 4042	Sheet 7	PARIS – ROUEN
GSGS 4346	K 55	OSNABRÜCK
GSGS 4346	L 53	HANNOVER

The Regiment landed in Normandy in three parties — A Squadron on 13th June, RHQ, B Squadron and part of HQ Squadron on 17th June and C Squadron and the remainder of HQ Squadron on 2nd July.

When the first two parties landed, the front line ran approximately as follows: - (Map 1/100,000 Sheet 7F Caen - Falaise)
including Cazelle 0276 - Cairon 9675 - Norrey en Bessin 9270 - Le Mesnil Patry 8970 - Christot 8770 - excluding St. Pierre 8568 - Hottot 8265.

49 Division (the bulk of whom had landed before the Regiment) had recently captured Christot and, a day or two after our landing, succeeded in occupying St. Pierre after a hard struggle.

For the first five weeks of the campaign, the Regiment was employed in a purely infantry role, for the majority of the time protecting the left flank of the Division and covering the gap between it and formations of first 1 and then 12 Corps on our left. We were at first based on Le Hamel 884706 and had the task of covering and patrolling into the long open cornfield that stretched southwards from that village for 3 to 4 kilometres; when the Division opened its attack on Fontenay 8767 and Rauray 8865 this task was performed by making a series of sweeps of the cornfield with carriers and assault troops which succeeded in inflicting considerable casualties on the enemy, although always bringing down heavy 88 millimetre fire on our own troops from the high ground east of Rauray. Meanwhile the left flank of the Division as it advanced was being protected by B sqn, under whose command was a troop of the Regiment's Anti-tank guns; when this troop reached the the eastern outskirts of Fontenay it spotted three Panther tanks emerging from a wood 500 yards to its front, and succeeded in knocking them all out; a fourth tank (a Mark IV Special) was later destroyed in the same area at very close range by a PIAT.

For the first three weeks of July there is little of interest to record; the Regiment, either as a whole or with its Squadrons under command of Brigade, held various parts of the line in the bridgehead or, more often, was in long stop positions behind the leading infantry and there was never during this period a chance for us to practise our normal role. On 24 July the Div was moved from 30 Corps area to the sector north and north east of Caen where it came under command of 1 Corps; here too the Regiment was disposed in an infantry role, with Squadrons under command of Brigades, and it was not until 15th August that we began to move forward and to do our real job of reconnoitring in front of the Division. The patrol reports during the previous night suggested that the enemy had withdrawn on our front to the high ground in the area of

Argences 1761 and the Regiment advanced on the right flank of the Division making rapid progress in spite of blown bridges and mines; enemy resistance was weak except on the line of the river Dives at Mezidon 2456.

These first two days were typical of our operations for the next fortnight, during which we led the advance of the Division to the river Seine at Quillebeuf (sheet 8E ref 7821). During this time we advanced approximately 50 miles and took 600 Prisoners of War; the enemy had destroyed all the bridges over all the rivers, but rarely put up any resistance except at these river obstacles, so that each day resolved itself into a rapid advance from a bridgehead secured by the infantry to the next obstacle where the process of examining the bridges and locating the enemy defences was repeated; by the time infantry came up we were able to give them a complete picture of the state of the obstacle and the positions held by the enemy so that they were able rapidly to cross the river and secure a foothold on the far bank for us once more to pass through. The line of our advance was from Mezidon on the river Dives via Rumesnil (sheet 7F reference 3167) and Bonnebosq 4395 to the river Touques at 5291 (sheet 8F); thence via St. Philbert 5694 to Cormeilles 6598 and the river Risle at Pont Audemer 7609 (sheet 8E). Only on this last stage was there any real opposition at any place other than a river obstacle; on 25th August the enemy made a determined stand in the area Epaignes (sheet 8F 7001) but were finally broken by the combined attacks of all three squadrons of the Regiment, who, with very little infantry support succeeded in inflicting over 100 casualties on the Germans; this was the last stand the enemy made south of the river Seine, and the river Risle was crossed both at Pont Audemer and to the south of the town almost without opposition.

The last eight miles to the Seine were covered in four hours, A Squadron reaching the river first at Quillebeuf and B Squadron shortly afterwards at Vieux Port 8316; during this one day 300 PW were taken, but this by no means accounted for all the German stragglers in the area for during the night of 27/28th of August A Squadron harbour at St Opportune 7915 was attacked by a large party of enemy who were probably trying to make their way to the river; the attack was successfully beaten off, and the next three or four days were spent in clearing the area, C Squadron in one day taking over 60 Prisoners of War in the Foret de Brotonne 91 through which they led 146 Infantry Brigade to the Seine at St Nicolas 9324.

On the last two days of the month, A Squadron succeeded in crossing the river Seine at Quillebeuf, getting first a reconnaissance patrol and later a larger force with vehicles over the river; no enemy were encountered, but great difficulty was found in dealing with the physical problems of the river crossing and only some 80 men and 12 vehicles could be ferried over in the class 5 rafts which were the only means available; as it was two carriers were lost owing to the rafts capsizing. However, those who crossed patrolled rapidly forward both in their vehicles and on bicycles provided by the civilian population and reached Bolbec 7533 Caudebec 9326 and St. Romain 6729 without incident. Further progress was not possible with the limited force available.

The attempt to ferry the entire Regiment over the river at Quillebeuf was abandoned and the whole unit, with the exception of that part of A Squadron which was already over, went round via Routot 9210 Grande Couronne 1205 Rouen 2013 (sheet 9E) and Duclair 0320 (sheet 8E) to Bolbec. The crossing of the river was made at midnight over the shattered railway bridge at Rouen 203132 all of which was in some degree broken and the northern span of which was leaning drunkenly into the river at a very steep angle; the bridge was littered with masses of smashed German equipment, motor transport and dead horses, barely allowing room for vehicles to pass, and the whole scene was illuminated by searchlights; a fantastic sight which for those who saw it is probably the most memorable of the whole campaign.

The crossing completed, our advance on Le Havre 5030 began; progress was at first rapid and no opposition at all was met until we reached the outer defences of the port. Some of these were quickly brushed aside (A Squadron captured an entire company on the morning of the 3rd of September) while much information was obtained about those which were too strong for us to destroy. As the infantry came up they took over from the Regiment, and assumed their dispositions for the assault on the town which was captured in a two day battle on 10 th - 12th September. The Regiment took no part in this assault but provided a Phantom wireless net of some 15 stations covering every unit participating, which materially assisted the Divisional Commander in his conduct of the battle, providing him with accurate and rapid information at every stage.

While the Division was engaged in the capture of Le Havre, the main stream of the advance of the Allied Armies had surged forward, engulfing the greater part of France and Belgium; we, left behind, had a few days rest near Bolbec and then in the area of Guerville M 5469 (1/250,000 GSGS 4042 sheet 4) before moving up on 21 Sep via Abbeville M 78, Arras H 50, Douai 70, Tournai and Brussels to the area Herenthout 9186 (1/100,000 GSGS 4336 sheet 3). There the Division· took over from 7 Armoured Division and on 23rd September the Regiment moved forward once more over the Albert canal, liberating Herenthals 9790 (where B Squadron built a bridge for themselves in order to get forward) and reaching the Turnhout canal on 24 September; on this day Turnhout

0506 was liberated, but all the bridges over the canal had been blown and no progress could be made until the infantry had secured a bridgehead and the sappers had built a bridge.

During the remainder of the month efforts were made to extend the bridgehead over the canal to the North East, North and West; the enemy clung tenaciously to his ground, and little progress was made except to the West where, after the capture of St Leonard 8709, troops of 2 Canadian Division were passed through; in the North, Ryckevorsel 9207 was liberated and from this base Squadrons, with the assistance of a Canadian Armoured Squadron, made a series of sweeps which, though they showed little result in territorial gains, succeeded in inflicting considerable casualties on the enemy; during the last seven days of the month well over 300 Prisoners of war were taken and many enemy killed.

On 3rd October the Division transferred its main weight from the Ryckevorsel area to that of Turnhout and, led by A Squadron, 146 Infantry Brigade advanced north on the road to Tilburg E 1532. A Squadron had a most successful day on the 5th October in the area Aerle 1123 where in a brief battle two troops destroyed two 88 millimetre and three 20 millimetre guns, took 10 prisoners of war and killed many more. C Sqn took over on 6th October in the area 1324, where they were strongly attacked by the enemy, but this attack was beaten off and many casualties were inflicted on the German paratroops engaged in it.

Between 7th and 18th October the Regiment was under command Bobforce, holding a line from Bolk 9612 via Ryckevorsel to St. Leonard; active patrolling produced a number of PW during this time but there were no offensive operations.

On 18th October the Regiment was withdrawn from Bobforce to form part of an armoured group consisting of this Regiment and 107 Regiment Royal Armoured Corps under the command of the Brigadier of 34 Tank Brigade and known as Clarkeforce. Between 20th October and 30th October this force advanced from Ryckevorsel to Kruisland (1/100,000 GSGS 2541 Sheet 4 reference 6935), a distance of some 25 miles, inflicting great damage on the enemy. Throughout the advance squadrons of the Regiment led the tanks into action, and had to fight their way forward against stubborn opposition from enemy infantry, paratroops and self propelled guns. The line taken was via Brecht 8410, Wustwesel 8115, Nieuwmoer 7619, Esschen 7323 and Wouw 6830 (1,100,000 GSGS 2541 Sheet 4) to Kruisland which was reached after the enemy had withdrawn from Roosendaal 7331 behind the Mark canal. During this advance most of the work had to be done on foot because of the extreme difficulty and open nature of the country; nevertheless progress was quite rapid and upwards of 150 prisoners of war were taken during the operation. In addition 30 more were taken when A Squadron swept the wood south of Nieuwmoer which had been by-passed and still contained enemy who had succeeded in capturing a considerable number of the Division's vehicles and men. During a three day lull at Nieuwmoer, C Squadron did some excellent patrolling north east of that village and directed our artillery on to many targets, while B Sqn were engaged in bitter fighting with enemy paratroops north of the village.

The enemy clung to the line of the Mark canal and a full scale infantry attack was necessary to dislodge him; as at Le Havre the Regiment manned a Phantom net to cover the battle. The Regiment had no operational commitments during the first fortnight of November except for a period of two days when A Squadron took over the area of Klundert 7845 from 104 US Division; on 13th November the Regiment moved east to the area Schaft (1/100,000 GSGS 4336 sheet 4 reference 4002) to join 12 Corps for operation Chester, designed to clear the enemy from the east bank of the river Maas and to capture Blerick E 9009 (1/250,000 GSGS 4042 sheet 3).

After 51 Infantry Division had secured a bridgehead over the ZIG canal, the Regiment was passed through on 18 Nov. For the greater part of the operations the Regiment was under command of 4 Armoured Brigade and, as in

Clarkforce, led the Brigade forward over very difficult country; progress was slow with the enemy hotly contesting every inch of ground and causing some damage with his self-propelled guns. However, the Regiment worked forward via Beringen 7103, Panningen 7704, Maasbree 8308 and Sevenum 8214 to the railway at 8315, whence Squadrons, pressing forward, reached Grubbenvorst 8915 on 25 November and the outskirts of Blerick 8911 on the same day, having covered 12 miles in the preceding week; very few prisoners of war were taken during this operation. The main problems during the advance were blown bridges, mines and considerable shell and mortar fire, and nearly all the work had to be done on foot.

On 29/30 November 15th Infantry Division took over in the Blerick area to enable this Division to move north to replace 50th Division on the island north of Nijmegen. The Regiment at first moved only to Mill E 6545 where it was held pending a decision as to whether or not it was to be used to quell civil disturbances in Belgium. As it was not required for this purpose one squadron was moved on 7th December to the extreme left flank on the Island in the area Hien 5870 (sheet 5) to come under command of a Brigade of 51 (Highland) Division and the remainder of the Regiment moved on 14th December to Druten 5368.

The flooding of the Island by the enemy compelled our troops to withdraw into a smaller bridgehead; 51st

Division was released from the area to join 30 Corps, and the Squadron at Hien came under command of the left hand Brigade of 49th Division on 26 December. Meanwhile, on 17th December, the remainder of the Regiment took over on the south bank of the river Waal between Druten and Wamel 4467 from 7 Canadian Reconnaissance Regiment, a task which was performed by one Squadron, the third being held in reserve in the area Leeuwen.

On the whole both Squadron fronts were quiet though both the enemy and ourselves patrolled actively on the Island, and clashes were frequent; clashes that took place were both between patrols and between our posts and enemy patrols; both sides suffered casualties and losses in these encounters, though at the end of our long stay in the area the score was definitely in our favour.

There was, of course, little or no patrol activity across the river Waal (which for the greater part of the time was in flood and difficult to navigate) although A Squadron had made an unsuccessful attempt to cross in the Leeuwen area in late January; this failed owing to the fact that the boats froze into the water and could not be moved. A second and completely successful attempt was made by C Squadron on 21st February; at 0100 hrs a party of approximately 30 men with two officers (including sappers and naval personnel) crossed from Druten to Ochten 5069 in two LCAs; the navy made a perfect land-fall, two patrols landed and after two hours ashore had inflicted considerable damage on the enemy; they returned at 0400 hrs with one dead enemy (from 34 Dutch SS Division), having suffered no casualties themselves. The operation had caused some misgiving in the planning stage owing to its unfamiliar nature and the physical difficulties of navigating the river, but it was extraordinarily successful in the event — a result that was largely due to the careful planning, preparation and training that preceded the actual operation and to the excellent co-operation of all arms — navy, gunners, sappers and our own men — in its execution.

Apart from this operation "JOCK", our activities were largely confined to observation post work and observed shooting, and to a considerable harassing fire programme every night; we had with us during the whole of our long spell on the Waal an RA HQ of our own, commanded by a Major with sometimes two and sometimes three officer assistants. The help they rendered was invaluable, dealing as they did with all gunner problems and arranging to bring down such fire as we desired. As to the guns themselves, we always had in support one troop of 25 pounders and two or three 17 pounder troops (the latter taking advantage of this opportunity to practise firing in a field role); in addition we also had, from time to time, troops of Bofors and 3.7 AA guns and platoons of 4.2 mortars and machine guns, all of which combined to make life as uncomfortable as possible for the enemy. There was little he could do in reply; apart from a good deal of Spandau fire, he had only a few mortars and some guns on the north bank of the Neder Rijn in the Rhenen 5076 area, none of which caused us much inconvenience, though he occasionally shelled the Island Squadron quite heavily.

This situation continued for over two months and it was not until 5th April that the Regiment was relieved from its commitments in an area in which we had been since early December 1944. Towards the end of this period, the Germans (or rather Dutch SS, for they were in front of us until the very end) became somewhat more active, and on one occasion caused much damage to the mortar position a mile west of Druten when they set their house on fire and burnt out seven vehicles. It was suspected that much of this activity might be attributable to agents living on the south side of the river (there was seldom any evidence of troops having crossed the Waal) but no proof of this could be given.

On the Island life was more varied for here contact with the enemy was possible without indulging in a major river crossing; of the many clashes that took place, perhaps the most memorable was that between a strong patrol of the Assault Company and an enemy party of eleven on 8th March, when, without loss to themselves, our men killed five and took prisoner four of the enemy. This was the first offensive operation in which the comparatively newly formed Assault Company had taken part, and its success was most gratifying.

These four months in a static role, during which the Regiment had never had an opportunity to perform its usual tasks or to do any mobile training (it was never relieved as a whole and the six day rest period which each Squadron regularly had in turn was always fully employed in maintenance and administration) did not augur well for the future; there had been so many changes, both in officers and other ranks since our last mobile operation in late November 1944 that the number of those who had taken part in a fluid battle was being steadily depleted, and it was at least a little doubtful whether, in any future operation, we could immediately attain our old standard of the Clarkforce and Blerick battles. When we were at last relieved, on 5th April, by a Belgian Fusilier battalion, the Regiment immediately went out on an exercise whose only fault was that it was shorter than could have been desired; owing to demands of maintenance and administration (and in particular vehicle loading) little time was available before we took part in the Division's assault on Arnhem 7577.

C Squadron, under command Division, had already on 3rd April been put across the Rhine at Emmerich to recce the country on the east bank of the Neder Rijn and Ijssel, but, owing to the rapid progress in that area of 2

Canadian Corps, there was little for them to do and on 4th April they returned to the Regimental concentration area. On 13th April the Regiment moved to a concentration area at Zevenaar 8669 (GSGS 4416 sheet P1 Bocholt) and on the 14th April crossed the Ijssel into Arnhem in order to pass through 146 Infantry Brigade and exploit northwards; on 16th April, Squadrons moved out and had a field day comparable with our best in France, taking 143 prisoners, killing many others and clearing the whole of the right flank of the Division — so much for our fears for their skill in a mobile role.

On 17th April the Division continued its advance west, and the Regiment, operating on its right flank again, quickly reached Lunteren 5589 without opposition (Map 1/100000 GSGS 2541 Sheet 2 Utrecht); from here C Squadron pushed out westwards and, advancing rapidly against light opposition (some enemy were killed and fifteen captured) seized the bridge at Renswoude 4988 intact after a brief struggle. To our sorrow, we were ordered to recall the Squadron by Division and the enemy reoccupied the bridge. The reason appeared later — partly in order to allow food convoys for the Dutch to cross the line and partly because negotiations for a German surrender were in progress, a Standstill Order had come into force on the Grebbe line; on 24th April the infantry (with one squadron under command of 147 Infantry Brigade) moved forward into contact with the line and there remained inactive; no offensive operations were conducted by either ourselves or the enemy and the situation remained unchanged until the final German surrender on the 4th May and our subsequent move forward into West Holland on the 7th to implement that surrender.

In the meantime, the Regiment had performed another mobile task which gave all of us the greatest satisfaction. On the 18th April the Regiment, less C Squadron, had concentrated in the area Otterlo 6591, C Squadron remaining at Lunteren under command of 147 Infantry Brigade; at 1630 hrs on that same day the Regiment was ordered by 1 Canadian Corps to move to Appeldoorn 7803 and to sweep the area bounded by the river Ijssel in the East and the Zuider Zee in the West — the Regiment to have under command a squadron of tanks, a battery of 25 pounders, a battery of 17 pounder self-propelled guns, a company of infantry and a platoon of Sappers and the whole group to be under Corps command, Division providing a No 12 set as rear link to Corps. This it is agreed is the ideal grouping against a retreating enemy and well within the scope of Regimental command and Signals. It is strongly felt that if a similar Regimental Group had been formed during the pursuit through France more casualties would have been inflicted upon the enemy and considerable time would have been saved. An Order Group was immediately called at Otterlo and orders for the move issued; by 2030 hrs the Group was concentrated at Appeldoorn, after a move of all but thirty miles; orders were issued and the start line crossed at 0815 hrs on the 19th — a performance of which we were justifiably proud.

The operation itself was little more than a triumphal march, for the Germans had unfortunately escaped by boat to Amsterdam some two days before: everywhere we were greeted with the greatest enthusiasm and by 1030 hrs A Squadron had reached Kampen 7641 (Sheet 2A) and B Squadron Nunspeet 6722 (Sheet 2); we remained in the area for two more days, collecting, during the whole operation, some eighty prisoners — some in hospital, some stragglers and others who were handed over by the Dutch Resistance.

On the 21st April the Regimental Group broke up, the Regiment returning to its old concentration area at Otterloo with one Squadron under command of the right Brigade, and the remainder resting, training and engaged in maintenance and administration. This state of affairs continued until the 7th May when we led the advance into West Holland, with A Squadron directed on Utrecht, B Squadron on Hilversum and Amsterdam and C Squadron on Baarn and Amersfoort. The Germans fulfilled their surrender conditions with correctness everywhere and no opposition was met; indeed the only impediment to our progress was the civilians, for it was only with the greatest difficulty that vehicles could force their way through the wildly enthusiastic crowds. All vulnerable points in the cities were seized by us and handed over to the Dutch Resistance, who, organized by the Squadrons, placed guards on them; in each town, Squadron Commanders ensured that the enemy fully understood their position and were complying with their orders, and in the evening handed over to the Infantry Brigades.

For the next four days Squadrons were decentralized under command of Infantry Brigades whom they assisted in escorting the enemy to their concentration areas; this task was completed by the evening of the 12th May by which time all German Divisional troops were disarmed and concentrated. There remained only the HQ, Signals and administrative companies of German 88 Corps which the Regiment itself disarmed and concentrated on the 13th and 14th May during which there passed through the disarmament area sixty officers, seven hundred and fortyone other ranks, three hundred and one Motor Transport and six Horse-drawn transport. The operation progressed smoothly and by midday on the 14th May the concentration was complete; Squadrons remained on guard over the Lager areas until relieved by 7 Canadian Reconnaissance Regiment of 3 Canadian Infantry Division on the 17th May.

On the 17th May the Regiment moved to a concentration area in the west part of Arnhem, from which it moved again via Zutphen, Enschede and Greven to a final concentration area south-east of Osnabrück (GSGS 4416 Sheet N 2 ref B 20) on the 23rd May when the Division came under command 1 British Corps. The whole Regiment was concentrated without difficulty in the village of Neuenkirchen 4493, where we awaited orders for our move to the area in which we should carry out our final task of the occupation of Germany.

49 (WEST RIDING) RECONNAISSANCE REGIMENT

MAP 1 : June 44 – August '44

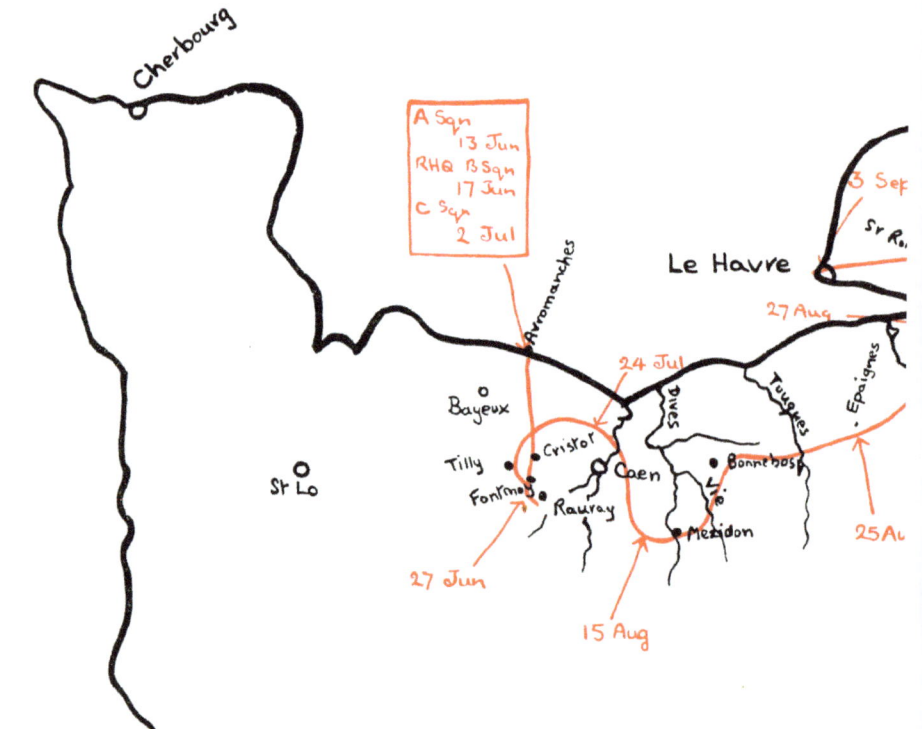

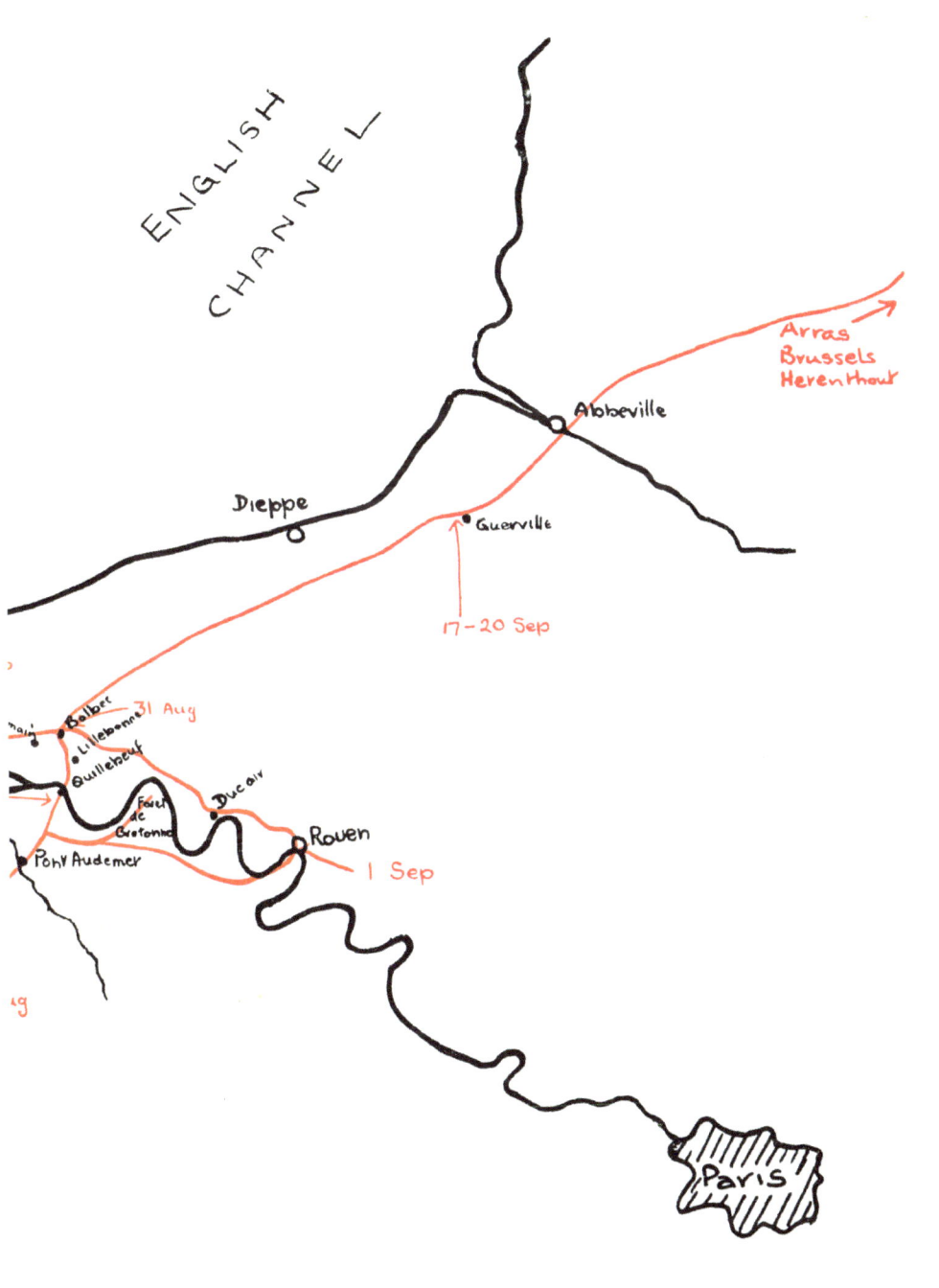

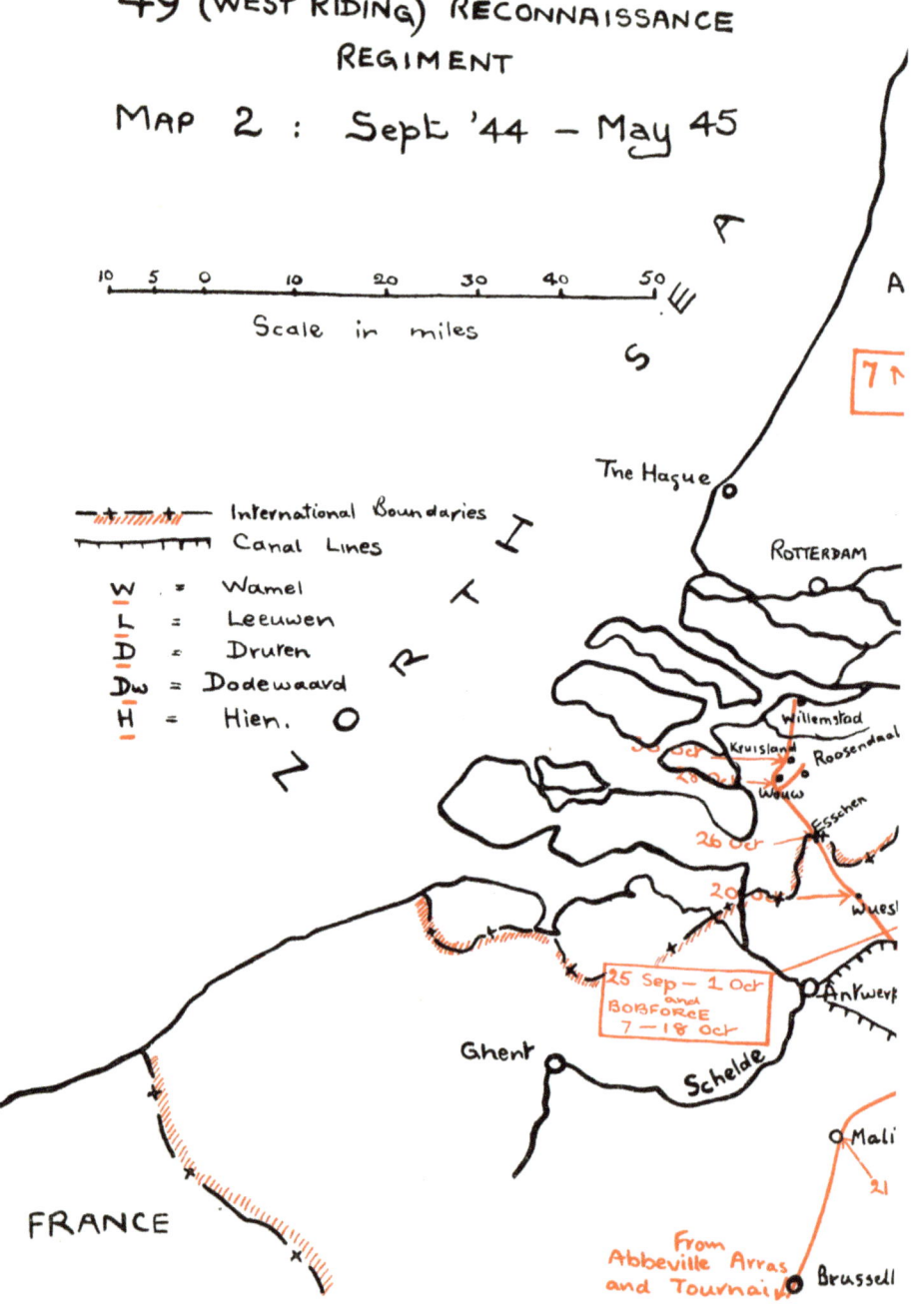

www.ingramcontent.com/pod-product-compliance
Lightning Source LLC
LaVergne TN
LVHW010309070426
835510LV00025B/3418